Feeding the Sloth

FEEDING THE SLOTH

SMALL STORIES WITH BIG IMPACT

Joe Scaggs

CONTENTS

Introduction

Why stories work, at work.

1. Feeding the Sloth   9

A Introduction to Unnecessary Complexities

2. Meatball Management   20

The Delicious Dilemma

3. Turning the Ship Around   26

Sales and Shuffleboards

4. The AutoDream Nightmare   34

Digital Disasters and Oversights

Introduction

Cross your fingers, and let's hope I've hit the mark here. If all goes according to plan, you'll find 'Feeding the Sloth and Other Parables' a refreshing departure from your typical, snooze-inducing business manual crammed with jargon. Instead, I've tried to spin a yarn or two, intertwining essential business and leadership principles with narratives that are as enlightening as they are engaging – and hopefully, a tad more entertaining than watching paint dry.

Imagine this as your expedition through a kaleidoscope of business concepts, minus the drudgery of your old college textbooks. We'll be skipping through the meadows of business strategy, customer engagement, and the often eyebrow-raising dynamics of sales and fulfillment teams. And don't worry, I've packed enough storytelling zest to keep you awake and maybe even chuckling.

My career's timing was as impeccable as a perfectly timed punchline. I dove into the professional pool during the splashy .com boom of the late 90s and swam through the murky waters of the Great Recession at a Fortune 10 financial giant.

I've dipped my toes in Banking, Insurance, Recruiting, Sales Management, Distribution, Finance, and Operations. I've crafted successful teams like a baker crafts a fine sourdough – with patience, mistakes and a bit of luck. My mentors were a mixed bag – some showed me the ropes, others showed me how to tie knots. Influential reads like "Who Moved My Cheese?" saved me from making blunders as a young exec.

And when I was a Senior Executive, "The Five Dysfunctions of a Team" was the secret sauce behind growing a business by 300% in a year. Let's not forget "The Goal," my north star in navigating operational efficiency at Angie's List.

Each chapter in this book is like a mini-safari, taking the theoretical beasts of business and turning them into relatable, domesticated creatures. It's like sweetening the pot of education, making the learning not just digestible but surprisingly tasty.

So, buckle up for a metaphorical rollercoaster sprinkled with humor. As you flip through these pages, you'll embark on a whirlwind tour into the heart of business and leadership, viewing these worlds through a lens of fresh, narrative-driven insight.

Gear up to plunge into a book that reimagines business learning as an exhilarating escapade, not a mundane march.

Welcome aboard a journey where the thrill of education meets storytelling!

Feeding the Sloth

Sam, a seasoned professional with experience in various fulfillment roles across both small and large organizations, now finds himself at the heart of a bustling rainforest. Tasked by a dedicated conservationist to ensure the health of an endangered sloth, he leads an eclectic team of sloth food gatherers. Approaching this unique challenge with vigor, Sam quickly sizes up the situation: A sloth is perched 30 feet up in the canopy, is apparently unresponsive to English or hand signals, and this sloth needs to eat.

With a sense of pressing urgency, Sam springs into action, formulating a meticulous plan. His first order of business is to have the team gather a diverse selection of leaves, shoots, and fruits, catering to the sloth's particular palate.

Showcasing his innovative spirit and keen intellect, Sam begins designing a delivery system that not only reflects his ingenious problem-solving skills but also holds the promise, albeit with some uncertainty, of successfully transporting the food up to the sloth's lofty abode.

Sam, known among his team for his plans that often teetered on the edge of genius and absurdity, had outdone himself this time with a contraption involving pulleys, ropes, computerized weight distribution, and a lot of wishful thinking.

The team, a mix of bright-eyed new recruits and seasoned veterans who had seen too many of Sam's 'brilliant ideas' go sideways, ventured deep into the forest.

They navigated treacherous terrain, occasionally stopping to question the life choices that led them here, to gather the finest sloth cuisine. Hours of labor later, they stood at the base of the tree, gazing up at their lofty customer, ready for the grand ascent of the feast.

Sam, with the confidence of a man who had never dropped an egg in an egg-and-spoon race, began the precarious hoisting of the food.

The team watched in a mix of awe and horror as the basket teetered upwards. Halfway up, in a moment that seemed to unfold with the dramatic flair of a telenovela, the branch holding the pulley snapped.

The basket of carefully selected delicacies descended in a spectacle of leaves and fruits, showering the forest floor and a particularly unamused armadillo.

The team stood in silence, the only sound being the soft thud of a mango making a late descent. Sam's face, a portrait of shock and dismay, slowly turned to meet the eyes of his team, who were now struggling to decide between a sympathetic pat on the back or a full-on intervention about his plan-making habits.

If at first you don't succeed…

Sam, the ever-optimistic manager, hatched a new plan that would show how much he was willing to work hard and bear adversity in pursuit of the goal. He ditched the pulleys and decided to deliver the collected gourmet meal to the sloth, in person.

He stuffed his pockets with the sloth's feast and began an ambitious climb. His team watched with bated breath and growing alarm. As Sam ascended, his pockets bulged comically with the green bounty. Birds paused mid-flight to witness this peculiar spectacle, and a curious monkey even followed him a few branches up, probably wondering if this human had finally lost it.

Then, at about 25 feet, just shy of his target, disaster struck. In a moment that would have made the most seasoned acrobat wince, Sam lost his grip. Down he tumbled, a whirlwind of limbs, leaves, and the occasional fruit making a cameo appearance. He landed with a thud that echoed through the forest, his pride taking the brunt of the fall.

Miraculously unharmed but with his dignity in tatters, Sam lay there, covered in a salad of rainforest delicacies. The sloth above watched with what could pass for slothful amusement, while Sam's team rushed to his aid, their faces torn between concern and the effort of not bursting into laughter.

As they helped him up, the forest floor was a mosaic of squashed fruits and trampled leaves, a testament to yet another of Sam's well-intentioned but poorly executed plans. The sloth, seemingly unphased, slowly moved to a more peaceful branch, probably pondering over the strange ways of the forest's two-legged inhabitants.

Sam found himself pondering the predicament. His task was simple yet challenging: to feed a sloth that resided high in the canopy. The previous attempts, marked by overcomplicated plans and comical misadventures, had taught Sam valuable lessons about simplicity and efficiency.

The third time? Use charm.

Dusting himself off, Sam had a different idea — one that required cooperation from an unlikely collaborator: the sloth itself.

As the sun cast dappled shadows on the forest floor, Sam approached the tree where the sloth, a creature of leisurely grace, hung lazily. He cleared his throat, feeling slightly ridiculous about to have a serious discussion with a sloth. "Mr. Sloth," he began, unsure if sloths had a preference for formal address, "I have a proposition that might interest you."

The sloth, with the slow, deliberate movements characteristic of its kind, turned its head towards Sam. Its eyes, reflecting a wisdom born of endless hours contemplating the forest's mysteries, seemed to encourage him to continue."

You see," Sam continued, "we've been trying to feed you in the most elaborate ways, and well, it hasn't been working out. I was thinking, what if we work together? Maybe you could come down a bit lower, and we'll bring the food closer to you. A joint effort, you know?"

The sloth blinked slowly, a gesture Sam optimistically interpreted as agreement. "Great!" he exclaimed, a bit too enthusiastically. "We'll get the food from just around here — fresh and delicious, I promise — and you won't have to wait in hunger while we bungle up another pulley system, and I won't have to break my neck with another free solo."

Sam and his team set to work, gathering the choicest leaves and fruits from the nearby flora. This time, there were no complex contraptions or precarious climbs. Just a simple collection of food and a short walk back to the sloth's tree.

True to their unspoken agreement, the sloth began a gradual descent, moving with a languid grace that belied its eagerness. As it reached a lower branch, close enough to the ground yet still comfortably aloft, Sam presented the day's bounty.

The sloth reached out with a slow but sure limb, its claws gently grasping a leafy branch offered by Sam. For a moment, human and sloth locked eyes, an unspoken understanding passing between them. It was a collaboration of sorts, one born of mutual respect and a shared goal.

As the sloth nibbled contentedly on its meal, Sam couldn't help but smile. He had learned an invaluable lesson: sometimes, the best solution is not about imposing one's own methods, but about finding common ground and working together.

This stark contrast sparked a lightbulb moment for the team, especially Sam, who mused that maybe, just maybe, not every problem required a Rube Goldberg machine to solve. They discussed the value of simplicity over complexity, a conversation peppered with jokes about their previous day's misadventure and suggestions for future sloth-feeding strategies, including but not limited to, a sloth food catapult.

In their reflection, they drew parallels to their professional lives. How often had they seen projects balloon in complexity, mirroring their pulley fiasco? The lesson was clear: sometimes the simplest solution is not only the easiest but the most effective, a principle that would resonate with anyone who's ever turned a straightforward task into an unintended adventure.

Think of a normal customer as a sloth - yes, a sloth! It is not much of a stretch. Sloths are laid-back creatures lounging in trees, much like how many businesses view their customers: seemingly passive and with sky-high expectations. However, here is the twist – not all customers are just hanging around with outlandish demands. Picture this: your customer, the sloth, is chilling up in the tree (probably contemplating the meaning of life), and along comes Sam and his team, embarking on an epic quest to deliver a gourmet meal right to its branch.

This whole adventure is a lot like what businesses go through to keep their customers happy. Sam's team, armed with determination and a map they can barely read, navigate the wild jungle of business processes and hurdles. They dodge low-hanging branches (unexpected challenges) and leap over muddy puddles (market changes) to deliver that five-star meal to our sloth friend.

So, remember, while our sloth customers might seem like they're just lounging about, waiting for greatness to fall into their laps, the reality is a high-flying adventure where businesses, guided by their inner Sam, go above and beyond to deliver value, one treetop at a time. And hey, who knows? Maybe your customer-sloth might just come down from that tree to give you a high-five (or a slow-motion thumbs-up, because, well, sloths!).

Sam, our resident fulfillment guru at Team Sloth HQ, has a job that is as challenging as trying to teach a sloth to sprint. Nevertheless, bless him, Sam sometimes thinks he's in a superhero movie, ready to save the day with over-the-top heroics. We will dive into the treacherous waters of 'Under Promising and Over Delivering' later, but for now, let us just say Sam's cape is a bit too tight.

Sam's plan? Go big or go home. Why collaborate when you can create a Rube Goldberg machine of fulfillment? He's keen on solving the puzzle, but overlooks that the sloth might just want to lend a paw.

In complex fulfillment environments, folks like Sam set the stage for fulfillment fiascos, where services and products arrive like a sloth on a leisurely stroll – slow and often off-course.

The moral of Sam's saga? Keep it simple; do not fall head over heels for your own grand plan.

Questions for the reader
In your organization, whom do you see as the sloth?
Who is Sam?

Meatball Management

In the heart of a quaint town, two Italian restaurants stood as culinary rivals: Mama Mia's, known for its traditional ambiance, and Pasta Perfection, the epitome of kitchen efficiency. At the center of this gastronomic rivalry was Emily, a local food blogger with an insatiable appetite for spaghetti and meatballs. Emily, a former amateur chef turned tech writer, had a knack for uncovering the hidden stories behind every dish.

Mama Mia's, once the crown jewel of the neighborhood, was facing a slow decline. Chef Antonio, a charismatic yet sometimes overzealous chef, had introduced bulk buying to cut costs and increase profitability.

He proudly switched to colossal 128-ounce cans of tomato sauce, which were more economical per ounce but far exceeded the restaurant's daily needs. The rationale was simple: the larger cans were $.12 cheaper per ounce of sauce and in a month the restaurant used a lot of sauce.

However, the kitchen only needed about 64 ounces per day. The leftover sauce, stored for use the next day, never tasted quite the same. The reheated sauce lost its freshness and vibrancy, leading to a subtle yet noticeable decline in the quality of the dishes. Customers like Emily, with a refined palate, noticed this change. The spaghetti and meatballs, once the highlight of Mama Mia's menu, now received lukewarm responses from diners.

Inevitably, some customers started to look for alternatives. This led to a decrease in profit for Mama Mia's. In an effort to drive the same top line revenue, Chef Antonio reluctantly raised the prices, unaware of the cycle of inefficiency he had set in motion. Now the customers faced with an increased price for a product declining in quality.

Pasta Perfection was the crosstown rival. Chef Amelia was fanatical about quality and the kitchen there ran on the principle of optimal efficiency. Chef Amelia focused on eliminating waste, not necessarily cost. They used 64-ounce cans of tomato sauce, perfectly aligning with the daily requirements.

This not only ensured zero waste but also guaranteed that each serving was made with fresh, high-quality sauce, a detail that did not go unnoticed by their customers.

As customers began to search for alternatives in the market, they fell in love with Pasta Perfection's Spaghetti and Meatballs. One of the many online reviews even read, "The sauce tastes just like Mama Mia's sauce, before they changed recipes.".

As demand grew, Pasta Perfection needed to add staff. Mario, the head cook at Mama Mia's and a veteran in Italian cuisine, decided to leave for Pasta Perfection. Chef Amelia, benefiting from its efficient operations and growing popularity, offered Mario a more lucrative package, a testament to Pasta Perfection's financial stability and commitment to attracting top culinary talent.

Mario's departure was the final blow to Mama Mia's. He had been the backbone of the kitchen, managing to maintain a semblance of order even amidst the chaos. His departure left a void that was hard to fill, further exacerbating the existing challenges.

As Mama Mia's struggled with its operational inefficiencies and the fallout from Mario's departure, Chef Antonio realized the need for change. He had been resistant at first, holding on to the belief that his bulk buying strategy was financially prudent. However, the combined impact of declining quality, rising prices, and the loss of his head cook forced him to reconsider his approach.

He began by addressing the tomato sauce issue, switching to smaller cans to ensure freshness. He reorganized the kitchen staff, streamlining operations to improve efficiency. These changes took time to implement, and the journey was not without its bumps. However, slowly but surely, Mama Mia's began to recover. The spaghetti and meatballs regained their former glory, the kitchen regained its rhythm, and the customers started to return.

Emily, on her next visit, was delighted to find her favorite dish restored to its old standard. Her blog post about Mama Mia's comeback, including a nod to Mario's move to Pasta Perfection, highlighted the dynamic nature of the culinary industry, where quality, efficiency, and talent are linked.

In the end, the story of Mama Mia's and Pasta Perfection became a lesson in the importance of adaptability, efficient resource management, and the need to prioritize quality over mere cost-saving measures. For Emily, it was a story of two restaurants' journeys, intertwined with her own culinary adventures, capturing the essence of a vibrant and ever-evolving food scene.

This story highlights a crucial lesson in business management: the difference between merely cutting costs and cutting waste. While cost-cutting focuses on reducing expenses, often at the expense of quality, reducing waste involves optimizing resources to improve both efficiency and product quality, ultimately leading to sustainable profitability and customer satisfaction. Mama Mia's and Pasta Perfection's contrasting approaches and subsequent fortunes underscore this critical distinction in the culinary world and beyond.

Questions for the reader
Do you use cost accounting in your business?

Will you stop using cost accounting as the primary decision-making component for your business? :)☐

Turning the Ship Around

Oceanic Voyages, a byword for opulence and thrill-seeking, found itself navigating troubled waters. Their once-celebrated paragliding excursions, the crown jewel of their experiences, had plummeted in terms of dependability due to a succession of mishaps.

A broken cable here, a late arrival there, and even a case where a customer ended up being ferried back to the wrong ship - these incidents were rare, but happened to be customers of the same booking agent, Larry Jackson.

The head of fulfillment for excursions, Jenny, had borne some of the responsibility for the errors. Despite refunding the affected passengers, the collection of issues drove a change in Larry's selling strategy. Larry, like all commission sales reps, sells where the compensation plan leads him. Refunds are a waste, and sales which refund aren't sales at all.

As a result of the situation, Larry began to gently nudge customers towards the more predictable yet mundane shuffleboard activities. Larry's compensation plan was structured to generate the same commissions whether the customer chose Paragliding or Shuffleboard.

Larry's sales narrative prioritized the reliability of shuffleboard over the exhilarating but perceived unreliable paragliding. "Avoid the letdown," he would say, half-jokingly, "Shuffleboard is where the true excitement lies!" The only letdown Larry was trying to avoid was on his commission report.

As Larry's peers saw his success they emulated the approach. This pivot, though minor on the surface, began reshaping Oceanic Voyages' very essence. As Oceanic Voyages shifted its bookings from the high-adventure paragliding to the more sedate shuffleboard, charter captains and harness masters sat idle, while the shuffleboard programs were overcapacity with participants.

The financial ramifications were significant and complex. In addition to waste from idle resources, a less apparent but painful realization began to emerge. As it turns out, Paragliding customers were more likely to select additional excursions after their exhilarating experience. Less Paragliders meant less booking for other excursions.

A Paragliding Enthusiast generated an additional 10% margin over a normal customer, and this extra profit was a crucial financial pillar for the company. The additional profit provided a substantial buffer, allowing Oceanic to fund various employee programs and charitable endeavors.

 These initiatives were more than just benevolent gestures; they were integral to Oceanic's brand image and market positioning as a company worthy of customer support and loyalty.

In contrast, shuffleboard customers rarely book additional excursions. While Shuffleboard offered a more reliable option and very few negative reviews, it was boring. The bored customers began to look to other provider at the port for their activities. The lower margin meant that every customer opting for shuffleboard over paragliding represented a direct hit to Oceanic's bottom line.

This shift had a cascading effect. With fewer funds flowing from the reduced margins, Oceanic found it increasingly challenging to maintain their employee programs and charitable activities at their previous levels. These programs were not just perks; they were a core part of Oceanic's identity and appeal. The cutbacks in these areas began to erode the company's reputation as a socially responsible organization, impacting their market image.

Moreover, the reduced financial cushion from the lower margins left Oceanic more vulnerable to market fluctuations and unexpected expenses. Where previously the higher margins from paragliding provided a safety net, the company now found itself operating with thinner financial buffers.

In summary, the shift from high-margin paragliding to lower-margin shuffleboard not only affected Oceanic Voyages' brand identity but also had significant financial implications. It strained the company's ability to support its valued programs and maintain its market image, highlighting the intricate balance between product offerings, financial health, and brand reputation in the business world.

An executive in the Finance department at Oceanic mistakenly concluded that customer preferences were changing and asked for a plan to pivot the company's marketing strategy to focus on low-adventure activities. This shift would be an inflection point for the organization built on adventure.

The CEO and founder, Daniel Ocean, decided to take a personal interest in the matter. Known for his hands-on approach and unexpected visits, Daniel booked a cruise under a pseudonym. He experienced firsthand the sales pitch from Larry, who, unaware of Daniel's identity, steered him towards shuffleboard with his usual charm.

Intrigued and slightly amused, Daniel played along but later revealed his identity in a dramatic fashion, right in the middle of a shuffleboard game. The revelation sent ripples of surprise and panic through the crew. Convening a meeting with Larry and Jenny, Daniel challenged them to identify the root cause of the shift away from adventure.

The meeting was a whirlwind of excuses, revelations, and a fair share of finger-pointing. Jenny admitted her lapses in fulfillment, while Larry confessed to his role in shifting towards perceived safer sales. Daniel, with a mix of sternness and wit, urged them to find a solution that would put the customers' desires for adventure back at the forefront.

Inspired and a bit chastened, Larry and Jenny devised a plan to revamp the paragliding excursion, ensuring its reliability and excitement. To test their efforts, Daniel himself decided to partake in the paragliding adventure. The image of the CEO, clad in a harness and soaring above the ocean, was both comical, inspiring, and created comfort and confidence for the team.

The trip was a success, and the photo of Daniel paragliding became the centerpiece of a new marketing campaign. "Experience the thrill of adventure with Oceanic Voyages," the ads touted, featuring a beaming Daniel in mid-flight.

The campaign was a hit, reigniting interest in the high-adventure excursions and bringing back the high-spending customers.

The sales team, motivated by the CEO's direct involvement and the renewed focus on customer experience, shifted back to promoting the full range of exciting excursions. Oceanic Voyages once again found its footing, balancing the thrill of adventure with the assurance of reliability, much to the delight of customers, who finally got their chance to fly, and to the relief of Larry and Jenny, who found a renewed sense of purpose in their roles.

The story of Oceanic Voyages sails us through the idea that Sales and Fulfillment, although often charting different courses in an organization, should ideally navigate the same waters. It casts a light-hearted beacon on the fact that when these teams are at cross-currents or when the communication lines are as tangled as fishing nets, it's not just a minor storm brewing – it's the customer experience that starts to sink. With a sprinkle of humor and a wave of insight, this narrative shows the importance of Sales and Fulfillment sailing in unison. They need to glide together like a well-coordinated paragliding team, maneuvering through the updrafts of incentive structures and the gusts of employee dynamics, all while keeping their sales strategies aligned with the customer's horizon.

This tale is a gentle reminder that when these departments soar in sync, it's not just smooth sailing – it's a successful voyage for the entire business.

Questions for the reader
What failures of communication led to this situation?
What could each department have done to avoid this in the future?
Do you have a sales rep in your organization who is selling against the current?

The AutoDream Nightmare

Nestled in the heart of a bustling Midwestern city, AutoDream Dealership stands as a testament to half a century of automotive excellence. Founded 50 years ago by a visionary entrepreneur, AutoDream quickly established itself as a cornerstone of the local community, its name synonymous with quality, reliability, and customer satisfaction.

Over the decades, AutoDream's reputation grew alongside its expanding inventory of cars. From classic sedans to modern electric vehicles, the dealership adapted to changing times while maintaining its commitment to top-notch service. Its showroom, a gleaming space always filled with the latest models, became a local landmark, a place where dreams on four wheels were realized.

The team at AutoDream, a blend of seasoned veterans and enthusiastic newcomers, shared a passion for cars and a dedication to customer service. Their deep-rooted understanding of the community's needs, combined with a genuine love for the automotive industry, drove the dealership's success.

Generations of families returned to AutoDream, trusting its expertise for their vehicular needs.

However, the evolving landscape of the automotive industry brought new challenges. The rise of digital platforms, changing consumer expectations, and the increasing complexity of car models demanded agility and adaptation. As AutoDream celebrates its 50th anniversary, the dealership confronts these challenges head-on.

Its story of success, resilience, and adaptation serves as the backdrop for a deeper exploration of the dynamics between sales promises, customer satisfaction, and the reality of fulfillment. In this chapter, we delve into the recent trials at AutoDream, understanding how a legacy of success meets the challenges of the present, and how this venerable institution plans to navigate the road ahead.

Rex, a seasoned sales manager with 30 years under his belt, has been a cornerstone of AutoDream's success. His charisma and deep knowledge of cars have endeared him to customers and colleagues alike. However, the rapidly changing landscape of car sales, especially the integration of online sales, presents a challenge even for a veteran like Rex.

The latest shift in AutoDream's sales model involves the dealership receiving cars that have been purchased online through the manufacturer's website. These vehicles, already sold to online customers, are shipped to AutoDream for final delivery. This system, designed to streamline the purchasing process, instead becomes a source of unprecedented chaos under Rex's watch.

Unfamiliar with the nuances of this new method, Rex, in his habitual enthusiasm to close sales, mistakenly sells these pre-purchased vehicles to walk-in customers. The confusion unfolds over a week, during which Rex unknowingly creates a tangled web of transactions, selling the same cars to multiple people.

Ashley, a bright-eyed young professional, represents the new generation of car buyers. She navigates the manufacturer's website with ease, excitedly selecting her first brand-new car. This purchase is more than a transaction for Ashley; it's a milestone, symbolizing independence and adulthood. She even returns her parents' old car, a gesture of moving on from her adolescent years. The day she is supposed to pick up her car from AutoDream, her anticipation is palpable.

On the other side of this scenario is Heather, a walk-in customer at AutoDream. She's decided it's time for an upgrade and chooses a car at AutoDream, the same one Ashley purchased online. Unaware of the mix-up, Heather trades in her old vehicle as part of the deal and drives off the lot in what she believes is her new car.

The collision of these two worlds occurs when Ashley arrives at AutoDream, only to find that her much-anticipated new car is gone, mistakenly sold to Heather. The disappointment and confusion hit her hard; she's now without a car, having returned her parents' vehicle in anticipation of her new purchase.

Heather's situation is equally distressing. She receives a call from AutoDream explaining the mix-up and requesting that she return the car. Bewildered and frustrated, Heather complies, but now finds herself without any transportation, her old car having been traded in as part of her now-void purchase.

This mishap at AutoDream spirals into a crisis, impacting not just the dealership's reputation but profoundly affecting the lives of its customers. Ashley's dream of driving her first brand new car with zero miles is shattered, and Heather is stranded without a vehicle.

The revelation of further errors hit like a storm. In a 24-hour period, Rex has sold 3 different online cars to walk-in customers.

Now four more customers find themselves in a similar predicament. Online buyers, who arrive at AutoDream brimming with excitement to pick up their new cars, grimace when they receive the news that their vehicles are in someone else's garage. Their anticipation quickly turns to frustration and anger, feeling betrayed by the system that was supposed to be seamless and reliable.

On the other side are the two additional walk-in customers, equally aggrieved. Having proudly driven their new cars home, they are contacted by AutoDream with the awkward request to return the vehicles. The embarrassment and inconvenience of this request leave them indignant, questioning the dealership's competence and integrity.

The fallout from this debacle is immediate and severe. Online reviews and local gossip paint AutoDream in an unflattering light, as a place where even the basic tenets of purchasing are mishandled. The situation also ignites internal turmoil, with staff members scrambling to rectify the mistakes and salvage the dealership's reputation.

In the wake of the chaotic missteps at AutoDream, the dealership scrambles to salvage its reputation and rectify the situation for the aggrieved customers. The management recognizes the severity of the error and the need for immediate action to prevent lasting damage to their long-standing reputation.

The dealership's first step is to extend an olive branch to Ashley, Heather, and the other affected customers. In a bid to make amends, AutoDream offers two years of free oil changes to each of them. This gesture, though well-intentioned, is met with mixed reactions. While some appreciate the offer, for others, it barely scratches the surface of the inconvenience and frustration they've experienced.

Behind the scenes, the administrative toll of correcting the error is significant. Staff members dedicate over 18 hours to untangle the web of paperwork and transactions caused by the mistaken sales. This intensive process involves reversing sales, reassigning vehicles, and managing the trade-ins, all while trying to maintain a semblance of normal operations at the dealership.

Despite these efforts, the damage to AutoDream's reputation begins to crystallize in the form of online backlash. Four stinging reviews appear across various platforms, detailing the mishap and expressing dissatisfaction with how the situation was handled.

These reviews, visible to a wide audience, cast a shadow over AutoDream's previously stellar reputation.
The long-term impact of this incident becomes apparent in the following years. Both Ashley and Heather, disillusioned by their experiences, decide to take their business elsewhere. Their departure is a symbolic loss for AutoDream - a sign that even decades of goodwill can be tarnished by a single misstep.

This incident at AutoDream highlights a crucial lesson for businesses in the digital age: the cost of sales operations errors extends far beyond immediate financial losses. The time and resources spent in rectifying mistakes, the challenge of restoring customer trust, and the enduring impact of online reviews pose substantial threats to any business, no matter how established it may be.

AutoDream's journey through this crisis serves as a stark reminder of the fragility of reputation and the need for adaptability and meticulous attention to operational details in a rapidly evolving market landscape.

Questions for the reader

What actions could AutoDream or the manufacturer taken to avoid this outcome?

What ways would they simplify the process of delivering the car to the online buyer?

Is Rex to blame for the situation?

Up the creek

Cliff, a seasoned senior executive, and Amy, his spirited junior counterpart, represented their company at this year's retreat. Their task was not just to network but to uphold the company's reputation in the most awaited event of the weekend: the canoe race.

As they approached the lake, the rival teams, all clad in their corporate colors, were already engaging in light-hearted yet competitive banter. Amid the laughter and camaraderie, there were subtle jabs and pointed remarks, particularly aimed at Cliff and Amy.

"You two better paddle as well as you sell," chuckled a rival from Acme Corp, a reference to the previous quarter's sales where Acme had just edged out Cliff and Amy's company. "Hope your canoeing is better than your numbers!" another chimed in from across the group.

Cliff, unphased, turned to Amy with a wry smile. "They think they've got us beat on the water just like they did last quarter. Let's show them that we're just as good with paddles as we are with sales pitches."

Amy nodded, her competitive spirit ignited by the friendly rivalry. "They won't know what hit them. It's not just about paddling; it's about strategy. And that's where we excel."The two walked towards their designated canoe, a sturdy yet unassuming vessel, laid out on the grassy bank. The lake's surface glistened under the morning sun, a perfect arena for the day's challenge.

As they prepared their canoe, the trash talk continued, each team boasting about their prowess both in the boardroom and on the water. But behind the laughter and jokes, there was an undeniable current of competition, a desire to outdo each other not just in sales, but in every aspect.

The stage was set, the teams were ready, and the air was filled with a mixture of competitive tension and the natural calm of the wilderness. For Cliff and Amy, it was more than just a race; it was a chance to prove their mettle, to show that they were as adept in handling physical challenges as they were in navigating the competitive world of sales.

As they pushed their canoe into the water, Cliff's last words echoed in Amy's mind, "Let's make this race a reflection of our next quarter – ahead of the pack and leaving everyone else in our wake."

With determined strokes, they began to glide across the water, ready to take on whatever the race, and their competitors, had in store for them.

The race commenced with a vigorous start, teams paddling furiously, slicing through the water's surface. Cliff and Amy, synchronized in their efforts, quickly took an early lead. Their strokes were strong and steady, propelling them forward with impressive speed. The cheers from the shoreline faded into a distant hum as they focused on the rhythm of their paddles and the calm, yet determined look in each other's eyes.

As they completed the first lap, their canoe seemed to glide effortlessly, cutting through the water like a knife through butter. Cliff's experience and Amy's vigor were a perfect combination, and they could sense the widening gap between them and their competitors. Confidence surged through them.

However, Amy's keen eyes soon noticed something amiss. A small but steady stream of water was seeping into the canoe. Her brows furrowed as she alerted Cliff, "We've got water coming in!"

Cliff spared a quick glance at the rising water at the bottom of the canoe but remained undeterred. With a reassuring grin, he replied, "The boat will be fine, at this pace we can win." His focus was unshakeable, his eyes fixed on the path ahead, the finish line already in his mind's eye.

Amy bit her lip, her gaze shifting between the accumulating water and the distant shoreline. The water was a minor nuisance now, but she knew it could become a significant problem if left unaddressed. Yet, Cliff's confidence was infectious, and his determination to win was clear. Trusting his judgment, she resumed her paddling, matching Cliff's strokes with renewed vigor.

Together, they surged ahead, the water in the boat sloshing rhythmically with their movements. The end was in sight, the cheers of the crowd growing louder with each stroke. But as they pushed forward, the water continued to rise, a silent threat that could undermine their strong lead.

Cliff's mantra of 'winning at all costs' echoed in Amy's mind as she paddled, a mixture of apprehension and adrenaline fueling her efforts. The race was more than a competition; it was a test of their resolve, a metaphor for their business challenges, and a reflection of their approach to problem-solving.

As they approached the halfway point, leading the pack, the question loomed large: Could they maintain their lead with the boat slowly filling with water, or would they need to rethink their strategy?

As the race progressed, the small trickle of water into the canoe had turned into a steady flow. Amy's concern grew with each stroke, her eyes darting between the rising water and the shoreline. "Cliff, we're taking on more water. We need to do something about this," she urged, her voice laced with anxiety.

Cliff, however, remained singularly focused on the race. Without missing a beat, he reached for his coffee cup tethered to the canoe, scooping up water and tossing it overboard. "This will keep us afloat," he declared, his tone exuding a mix of determination and denial.

But with every cupful of water Cliff scooped out, his paddling slowed. The rhythm they had established was broken, and their speed began to decrease. Amy's paddling alone couldn't compensate for the loss of momentum. Their lead started to diminish as rival canoes began to close the gap.

Amy watched in frustration as the other teams, once far behind, started to inch closer. "Cliff, we're losing our lead. That cup isn't enough," she exclaimed, her voice tinged with desperation.

Cliff's eyes remained fixed on the water inside their canoe, his actions becoming more frantic. With each passing moment, the reality of their situation became more apparent. Finally, as another team drew level with them, Cliff's resolve faltered. "We need a bigger cup," he muttered, the futility of his solution dawning on him.

The irony of the situation was not lost on Amy. Here they were, leaders in their field, reduced to bailing out a sinking canoe with a coffee cup, while their competitors capitalized on their dilemma. The metaphor was painfully clear: focusing on short-term fixes without addressing the underlying issue was a recipe for disaster.

As they continued to lose ground, Amy's mind raced for a solution. The race was slipping away from them, just like their competitive edge in the market could if they didn't change their approach. It was a lesson in real-time, a vivid illustration of the consequences of neglecting fundamental problems in favor of quick fixes.

But could they adapt in time to salvage the race, or would they be left to ponder their mistakes as their rivals sailed past them?

As Cliff and Amy struggled with their predicament, the first of their competitors, a sleek red canoe from DynaTech, glided past them with ease. Its occupants, focused and determined, barely glanced at Cliff and Amy's floundering vessel. Cliff, in a moment of desperation, called out to them, "Hey, can you spare a bigger cup or something?

"The DynaTech team, intent on their own race, didn't respond. They were a well-oiled machine, their paddles cutting through the water in perfect harmony, exemplifying the focused drive that had made them formidable in the business world.

Cliff's frustration mounted, but before he could dwell on it, another competitor approached. This time it was a team from GlobalTech, known for their aggressive tactics in the market. Sensing weakness, they saw an opportunity. As Cliff repeated his plea, this time for a bucket, one of the GlobalTech paddlers, with a mischievous grin, began splashing water into Cliff and Amy's already beleaguered canoe.

Amy's face was a mix of disbelief and anger as their situation worsened. "Enough, Cliff! We need to fix this ourselves," she declared, steering their canoe towards the shore. Cliff, still clutching his now useless coffee cup, seemed lost in thought, unable to let go of his ineffective solution.

Their canoe, heavy with water, struggled to make it to land. Just as they neared the shore, the vessel bottomed out, the front of the canoe digging into the mud. They were so close, yet so far. Waterlogged and defeated, they clambered out of the canoe.

Cliff, ever the optimist even in the face of obvious failure, quickly formulated another plan. "Quick, let's empty out the water and get back in the race," he said, his voice tinged with a mix of hope and urgency.

Amy looked at him, then at the distant canoes now far ahead, and then back at their sunken canoe. The absurdity of the situation was almost comical. Here they were, supposed leaders in their field, now literally stuck in the mud, their competitors having turned their misfortune into their own advantage.

It was a moment of reckoning for both of them. As they began to bail out the water, the futility of continuing the race in their current state was palpable. The lesson was clear: without addressing the root cause of their problem, they were doomed to repeat their failure, in this race and perhaps in the business world too.

The real challenge now was not just about getting back into the race, but about understanding and addressing the fundamental issues that had led them to this point. It was a lesson in humility, strategy, and the importance of proactive problem-solving, delivered in the most unexpected of ways.

As Cliff and Amy frantically worked to empty their canoe, the hole that had been a mere nuisance at the start had now grown significantly. The constant pressure from the water and their desperate attempts to stay afloat had only worsened the situation. And when their boat had bottomed out in their rush to the shore, the hole had become a gaping wound in the vessel's hull.

The task of patching up the canoe, which would have been simpler at the onset of their troubles, was now a monumental challenge. Time seemed to stretch as they labored over the repair, with the sounds of the ongoing race echoing mockingly in the background. Every minute spent patching up the hole felt like an eternity, knowing that with each passing moment, their competitors were drawing closer to the finish line.

Finally, after what seemed like an age, they managed to patch the hole, albeit imperfectly. They pushed their canoe back into the water, their movements reflecting a mix of determination and resignation. As they resumed paddling, their strokes were less about winning and more about completing what they had started.

Back on the water, Cliff and Amy struggled to catch up. They paddled with a sense of urgency, but the lost time and energy were impossible to recover. The once-leaders now trailed behind, their efforts a stark contrast to the spirited start they had made.

As they crossed the finish line, long after the other teams had completed the race, there was a sense of subdued accomplishment but also of missed opportunity. Cliff, his face a mixture of exhaustion and frustration, was quick to blame their misfortune. "Faulty equipment," he grumbled, shaking his head. "We could have won if not for that."

Amy, however, was deep in thought. As they pulled their canoe ashore, her mind wasn't on the hole or the water or even the race itself. It was on Cliff's reaction, on his readiness to blame external factors without acknowledging his role in their predicament. The whole experience, from the race to the sinking to the patching up, seemed to her a metaphor for how they approached challenges in their work.

She wondered if Cliff understood the real lesson from today. It wasn't just about the hole in the boat or the competitors who had capitalized on their weakness. It was about recognizing problems early, taking responsibility, and addressing them before they escalated. It was about leadership, foresight, and the willingness to adapt and change course when needed.

As they packed up their gear, the day's events replayed in Amy's mind. The race was over, but its lessons lingered, offering insights not just for their business strategies but also for their personal growth as leaders and team members.

The retreat had been more than just a corporate event. It had been a reflection of their approach to challenges, a mirror showing them not just their strengths but also their weaknesses. And for Amy, it was a starting point for a conversation, a chance to share her thoughts with Cliff, hoping he too would see the broader implications of their day on the lake.

Questions for the reader
What could Amy have done differently in the situation?
Is Cliff a typical Sales Executive?

Pinata Promises

In the whimsical town of Progressville, nestled among streets lined with confetti trees, stood "Joyous Jamboree," a company whose party supplies could make even the dullest day dazzle. Their most enchanting item? The Magical Piñata, known to be the life of any party.

The head of fulfillment at Joyous Jamboree, Mr. Fernando Fasttrack, was a man with a plan. His motto, "Underpromise, overdeliver," was more than just words; it was the rhythm to which the entire fulfillment department danced. Fernando believed in setting timelines so comfortably long, they could vacation in them.

Enter Mrs. Garcia, a mom on a mission to procure a Magical Piñata for her son's birthday. She approached a sales rep, eager to place her order. The rep, bound by Fernando's over-cautious timelines, regretfully informed her that the delivery would take a whole five days.

Little did Mrs. Garcia know, the fulfillment team at Joyous Jamboree operated like a well-oiled, albeit slightly overzealous, machine. The moment her order was placed, the Piñata Squad sprang into action, crafting and packaging her order with the speed of a thousand party poppers.

Contrary to the promised timeline, the piñata was ready to be shipped in just three days. Fernando, proud of his team's efficiency yet adherent to his policy, dispatched the order, expecting Mrs. Garcia to be pleasantly surprised by the early delivery.

However, Progressville's weather had other plans. As the delivery van, adorned with banners reading "We bring the party to you!" made its journey, a rogue rainstorm, notorious in local folklore as "The Spoilsport Sprinkle," decided to make an untimely appearance.

Mrs. Garcia, having taken Fernando's five-day timeline seriously, was out with her son, leaving the Magical Piñata to fend for itself against the elements. When she returned, she discovered the piñata looking more like a soggy cereal flake than a beacon of birthday joy.

The aftermath was a mix of bewilderment and laughter. Mrs. Garcia, ever the optimist, found humor in the piñata's plight, while Joyous Jamboree learned a valuable lesson.

After the soggy piñata incident, Fernando Fasttrack, the head of fulfillment, decided it was time for a change. Instead of improving communication on realistic timelines, he took a different route: aligning the fulfillment process precisely with the promised five-day schedule.

Gone were the days of the fulfillment team's lightning-fast efficiency. The new mandate was clear: match the delivery precisely to the five-day expectation. This shift led to an unexpected transformation within the team.

One afternoon, in the once bustling warehouse, now a haven of leisurely paced work, Mike, a member of the Piñata Squad, lounged on a stack of bubble wrap, casually chatting with a colleague. "You know, I used to pack these piñatas like there was no tomorrow. Now? We've got all the time in the world. This one?" He patted the piñata next to him, "Not due for another four days. Easy peasy."

However, complacency often invites chaos. On the fourth day, a critical packaging machine decided to take an unscheduled break, halting the entire process. The team, now unaccustomed to urgency, scrambled to fix the issue. The piñatas, which could have been ready days ago, were now in danger of missing their delivery dates.

Meanwhile, at the sales front, a new customer, Mrs. Lee, urgently needed a Magical Piñata for her daughter's birthday party in three days. The sales rep, bound by the new five-day policy, regretfully informed her that it couldn't be done. Mrs. Lee left, disappointed, taking her business to a rival company that promised a faster turnaround.

The consequences of Fernando's decision rippled through Joyous Jamboree. The missed delivery and lost sale were wake-up calls. The team realized that their previous efficiency wasn't just about overdelivering; it was a buffer against unforeseen circumstances and a competitive edge in the market.

Fernando, witnessing the fallout, understood the error in his approach. Slowing down operations to match extended timelines had bred complacency and stripped the team of its proactive spirit. He called a meeting, admitting his mistake.

One sunny afternoon, a crucial meeting took place between Fernando and the sales team. The topic? Realigning their strategies to better serve customer needs. "It's clear," Fernando began, "that we need to sync our efforts. Our goal isn't just meeting timelines; it's about being responsive to what our customers actually need."

"Team, I thought I was helping by easing our pace, but I see now that our strength lies in our agility and readiness. Let's find a middle ground. We need to be efficient but also flexible enough to adapt to the unexpected. Let's set realistic timelines, but keep our spirit of excellence. We're not just fulfilling orders; we're delivering joy, and sometimes, joy can't wait."

The change was swift and significant. Sales and fulfillment started collaborating closely, tailoring their efforts to the specifics of each order. This new synergy was soon put to the test when Mrs. Davidson, a new customer, called with an urgent request."

I need a Magical Piñata for my son's party in two days. I know it's a tight timeline, but I'm willing to pay extra for expedited service," she explained anxiously.

The sales rep, now empowered to work closely with fulfillment, quickly relayed the request. Fernando, embracing the new approach, rallied his team. "We have a challenge, but also an opportunity. Let's show what we can do when we work in unison!"

The fulfillment team, rejuvenated by the challenge, sprang into action. The piñata was crafted, packaged, and ready to go in record time. The delivery, made with a day to spare, left Mrs. Davidson delighted and grateful.

This success was more than just a timely delivery; it was a testament to the power of alignment between sales and fulfillment. The newfound efficiency and adaptability led to increased customer satisfaction, and word spread about Joyous Jamboree's remarkable ability to meet even the most pressing demands.

Fernando reflected on this turnaround. "By aligning our efforts and focusing on what the customer really needs, we've not only become more efficient but also more relevant. We're not just a company that delivers piñatas; we're a team that delivers happiness, on time, every time."

Joyous Jamboree's reputation soared. Customers appreciated the company's responsiveness and flexibility, leading to an increase in both orders and customer loyalty. The Magical Piñata, already a symbol of joy, became synonymous with reliability and exceptional service.

The story of Joyous Jamboree's transformation spread throughout Progressville, serving as a shining example of how understanding and meeting customer needs, through a harmonious alignment of sales and fulfillment, can lead to success and efficiency in business.

Questions for the reader
Do you think 'underpromising and overdelivering' is just as disruptive as 'overpromising and underdelivering'? Does your organization have healthy fulfillment buffers? Were these buffers originally created to avoid friction, but are now crutches for laziness and sources of complacency?

Jargonauts

In the heart of a bustling space center, nestled among towering launch pads and buzzing control rooms, stood the Star Voyager – a spacecraft that looked like a committee of children with an unlimited budget had designed it. Its sleek, silver body gleamed under the sun, proudly displaying every antenna, solar panel, and inexplicably placed bulbous module, as if it were trying to win a space fashion show.

The mission was simple, at least on paper: travel to the outer edges of the solar system, conduct a series of 'very important scientific experiments', and return safely. The kind of mission statement that sounded reassuringly straightforward, until you remembered it involved hurtling through the cold, unforgiving void of space in a vessel made by the lowest bidder. Around the Star Voyager, the space center was a hive of activity.

Engineers scurried around with clipboards, looking important. Technicians adjusted things that seemed already perfectly adjusted. And somewhere in the mix, a tour group of school children, all wearing oversized space helmets, were asking questions that nobody had answers to, like "Why doesn't the spaceship have wings?" and "Can it do a loop-de-loop?"

Somewhere above this orchestrated chaos, in the control room, mission directors with headsets were engaged in serious-looking conversations, occasionally glancing at the large digital countdown clock that dominated one wall. They spoke in that unique blend of jargon and acronyms that could either be discussing complex space maneuvers or ordering a particularly complicated coffee.

Meanwhile, the Star Voyager's crew was preparing for the journey of a lifetime, blissfully unaware of the minor panic their pending departure was causing among the ground staff. Little did they know, their voyage would be anything but routine, and their biggest challenge wouldn't come from the depths of space, but from within their own ship.

Captain Greta Proton was not your typical astronaut. If you asked anyone at the space center, they'd tell you that Greta had been born with rocket fuel instead of blood in her veins. She had the kind of resume that made you wonder if she ever slept: multiple missions to the International Space Station, a stint on the Moon, and she even held the unofficial record for the most freeze-dried ice cream consumed in zero gravity.

Greta was a living legend, the kind who casually mentioned spacewalks like they were strolls in the park. She was as unflappable as they come, with a demeanor so calm and collected it made cucumbers look stressed. Her crewmates often joked that if Greta ever wrote an autobiography, it would be titled, "Space: It's Just Not That Big a Deal."

But it wasn't just her stellar (pun intended) career that set her apart. Greta had a sense of humor as dry as the vacuum of space. She could defuse tension with a well-timed joke, and her laughter was known to echo through the corridors of spacecrafts, making even the most mundane tasks seem like fun.

On this particular mission, Greta was both captain and mentor. She had seen it all, from minor glitches to full-blown emergencies, and had a knack for solving problems with a mix of ingenuity, duct tape, and an unwavering belief that there was no situation that couldn't be improved with a good cup of coffee.

Greta's backstory was as colorful as her personality. Raised by two astronomers, she often joked that she had been taught to navigate by the stars before she learned to walk. Her childhood was filled with star charts, telescopes, and camping trips where bedtime stories were replaced with lessons on constellations.

As she stood in the Star Voyager, checking systems and prepping for takeoff, Greta couldn't help but feel a familiar thrill. It didn't matter how many times she left Earth's atmosphere; the excitement never faded. And on this mission, she had the added challenge of guiding a rookie astronaut, someone who was about to learn that space travel was nothing like the movies. But Greta was ready. After all, if you can teach a group of rowdy schoolchildren about the Orion Nebula, guiding a newbie through their first space mission should be a walk in the park. Or, more accurately, a float in space.

Enter Jeff Reynolds, the newest addition to the spacefaring team. Jeff was the epitome of a rookie astronaut: bright-eyed, bushy-tailed, and with a tendency to get overly excited about anything that beeped or flashed inside the spacecraft. If enthusiasm could be converted into rocket fuel, Jeff would have single-handedly powered the Star Voyager to Pluto and back.

Unlike Greta, Jeff's journey to becoming an astronaut was less of a straight shot to the stars and more of a scenic route. Originally a software engineer, Jeff had spent the better part of his career writing code for satellite navigation systems. He loved his job, but he often found himself gazing out of his tiny office window, daydreaming of being among the stars rather than just writing software for them.

Jeff's backstory was a charming tale of perseverance and slightly questionable decision-making. After watching a particularly inspiring documentary about space travel, he impulsively decided to apply for the astronaut program. To the surprise of everyone (including himself), he was accepted. The selection committee later admitted they were impressed by his unique combination of technical expertise and, as they diplomatically put it, "unbridled enthusiasm for space."

In person, Jeff was like a human golden retriever: loyal, eager, and always ready for an adventure. His training had been rigorous, pushing him to the limits physically and mentally, but nothing could dampen his spirits. If anything, each challenge only made him more excited for the journey ahead.

As the launch day approached, Jeff's excitement was palpable. He was like a kid on Christmas morning, if Christmas involved strapping yourself to a giant rocket and hurtling into the cosmos. His colleagues had taken to affectionately calling him "Starstruck" due to his habit of getting lost in thought while staring at the spacecraft.

But for all his excitement, Jeff was also acutely aware of his inexperience. He knew that space travel was serious business, and while he had the technical skills, he lacked the practical experience of someone like Greta. Fortunately, Jeff was a quick learner and more than willing to soak up every bit of wisdom Greta was willing to share. He saw this mission as his big chance to prove that he was more than just a space enthusiast – he was a bona fide astronaut. And he was determined not to let anything, not even his own nerves, get in the way of that.

The final hours before the launch were a symphony of controlled chaos inside the Star Voyager. The spacecraft was alive with the hum of machinery, the occasional beep of computers, and the soft murmur of the crew making their last-minute checks. Every surface seemed to twinkle with indicator lights, creating a tableau that would have made any Christmas tree green with envy.

Jeff buzzed around like an electron in an excited state, double-checking his equipment, re-reading the mission manual for the umpteenth time, and asking Radaris, the onboard AI, a barrage of questions. His movements were a dance of anticipation and nerves, his face a canvas displaying a spectrum of emotions, from wide-eyed wonder to fleeting moments of doubt.

Greta, on the other hand, was the picture of tranquility amidst the whirlwind of activity. She moved through the spacecraft with the grace and assurance of someone who had done this many times before. Her presence was like a calming balm, her voice steady and reassuring as she went over the final procedures with the crew.

As the countdown began, the energy inside the Star Voyager shifted. The reality of what was about to happen settled over everyone like a tangible cloak. Greta took her position in the captain's chair, her fingers deftly moving over the control panel. She glanced over at Jeff, who was now strapped into his seat, his eyes fixed on the console in front of him.
"Remember, deep breaths," Greta said with a smile, "Space doesn't care how fast your heart is beating, but it helps if you can keep your cool." Jeff nodded, trying to mirror her calmness. His heart was racing, a drumbeat of excitement and anxiety. This was it, the moment he had been dreaming of since he first looked up at the stars as a child. He could feel the weight of the moment, the culmination of years of hard work and dreams.

The final countdown began, and the voice of mission control filled the spacecraft. "T-minus 10 seconds to launch." Jeff's grip tightened on the armrests, his knuckles turning white. He could feel the rumble of the engines coming to life, a deep, resonant sound that seemed to vibrate through his very bones.

Greta's voice cut through the mounting tension. "Ready for the ride of your life, Jeff?" she asked, her eyes twinkling with a mix of excitement and confidence. Jeff managed a nervous smile. "As ready as I'll ever be, Captain."The final seconds ticked away. "Three... two... one... liftoff!"

The moment the countdown hit zero, the Star Voyager transformed from a silent, gleaming monument of human engineering into a roaring beast of power and energy. The engines ignited with a fury that shook the very air around them, a thunderous crescendo that drowned out all other sounds, a physical manifestation of humankind's audacity to reach for the stars. Jeff felt a sensation unlike anything he had ever experienced. It was as if an invisible giant had grabbed hold of the spacecraft and was propelling them upwards with unstoppable force.

The pressure was immense, pressing him back into his seat with a weight that seemed to increase by the second. It was exhilarating and terrifying in equal measure, a rollercoaster ride with no equal. In that moment, all of Jeff's anxieties melted away, replaced by an overwhelming sense of awe.

They were heading into the unknown, into the vast expanse of space, and he was part of it. He tried to turn his head, to catch a glimpse of the Earth through the windows, but the force of the launch made even the smallest movements a Herculean effort. Through the window, he could see the Earth falling away, becoming a beautiful, swirling marble of blues and greens.

He turned to look at Greta, who focused on the panels in front of her, but there was a small, satisfied smile on her lips. She caught his gaze and nodded a silent message of encouragement. Jeff nodded back, feeling a newfound sense of confidence. He was ready for whatever lay ahead, ready to face the challenges of space. With Greta at the helm and the stars as their destination, the possibilities were endless.

As the Star Voyager ascended, the roar of the engines filled every corner of the cabin. Jeff could feel the vibration in his bones, a constant, thrumming reminder that they were leaving the familiar behind. Finally, as they broke through the atmosphere, the resistance eased, and the crushing pressure gave way to a surreal weightlessness. The roar of the engines faded to a distant hum, and the chaotic vibrations smoothed into a gentle, almost soothing rhythm.

Jeff turned his head and looked out of the window. The sight that greeted him took his breath away. Earth, once so vast and all-encompassing, was now receding into the distance, shrinking into a beautiful, fragile-looking orb suspended in the infinite blackness of space.

The blues of the oceans were more vivid than he had ever imagined, the swirls of clouds more mesmerizing. It was a view he had seen in countless pictures and videos, but nothing could have prepared him for the experience of seeing it with his own eyes. Beside him, Greta was the picture of composure. Her hands moved with practiced ease over the controls, adjusting the spacecraft's trajectory and monitoring the various systems. Her face was calm, her focus unwavering, but there was a glint in her eye, which bespoke her own appreciation for the beauty outside their window.

As the Star Voyager continued its journey, leaving Earth and its mysteries behind, Jeff knew that this was more than a mission. It was an odyssey, a voyage into the unknown, with the vast expanse of space as their canvas and the stars as their guide. The adventure had truly begun.

Two weeks into their voyage, with the vastness of space enveloping the Star Voyager, an unexpected emergency jolted the crew from their routine tasks.

The spacecraft trembled slightly, and a series of alarms blared throughout the cabin, signaling a critical fault in the electrical system that controlled the life support. Red lights flashed urgently, casting an ominous glow over the interior.

Jeff felt a surge of panic as he stared at the control panel, its lights blinking in a chaotic dance. "What's going on?" he stammered, his voice laced with anxiety.

Captain Greta Proton, with her usual calm demeanor, quickly assessed the situation. "It's the life support's electrical system," she announced, her fingers moving deftly over the controls.

Jeff: (Urgently) "Radaris, initiate a full diagnostic. We need to communicate with Earth's technical team immediately."

Radaris: (In its unflappable AI voice) "40 minutes until life support failure. Commencing diagnostic now."

As Jeff and Greta wait anxiously, Radaris completes its diagnostic.

Radaris: "Diagnostic complete. Life support system failure imminent. Earth's technical team appears to be referencing the updated technical manual, which has not been integrated into my database."

Jeff: (Frantically speaking into the communicator) "Earth, this is Star Voyager. We have a critical life support issue. Radaris can't comprehend your instructions. We need clear guidance, and fast!"

Jeff: (Anxiously speaking into the communicator) "Star Voyager to Earth's technical team, we've got a critical situation with our life support system. Radaris just confirmed it's failing. We need immediate assistance."

Time passes as they wait for a response, the silence heavy with tension.

Earth's Technical Team: (Static crackles before the message comes through) "Star Voyager, we copy. Please initiate protocol Alpha-9 and reroute the flux capacitance through the quantum manifold. Ensure the hyperbolic paraboloid is in sync with the tachyon emitter. Over."

Jeff frowns, trying to process the instructions.

Jeff: "Earth team, can you simplify that? I'm not familiar with a 'hyperbolic paraboloid' or how to sync it with a 'tachyon emitter.' We need clearer instructions. Time is critical!"

Another delay as Earth's response is awaited, adding to the frustration.

Earth's Technical Team: (After a lengthy pause) "Star Voyager, affirm rerouting the flux capacitance. The hyperbolic paraboloid is the curved interface on the emitter. Adjust its frequency to match the tachyon pulses. It's critical for stabilizing the quantum field. Over."

Jeff, exasperated, turns to Greta. "Do you have any idea what they're talking about? This is like deciphering an alien language. And with this time delay, it's just making things worse!"

As the minutes ticked by, the situation aboard the Star Voyager grew increasingly critical. Every delay, every miscommunication with Earth, compounded the problem. It was a race against time, and they were losing.

Just as the situation seemed almost hopeless, a new voice crackled through the communication system. "Star Voyager, this is Roger.

I'm on orbital station in the Asteroid belt. I just overheard your situation. Maybe I can help." Roger's voice was a lifeline in the darkness. Unlike the technical team on Earth, he spoke in clear, jargon-free language, making the complex instructions accessible to Jeff. He patiently guided Jeff through the repair process, his explanations straightforward and easy to understand.

With Roger's guidance, Jeff found his confidence growing. The overwhelming instructions began to make sense, and he worked swiftly to implement the necessary repairs. Greta, meanwhile, coordinated with Roger and monitored the spacecraft's systems, her expertise invaluable in managing the crisis.

The collaboration between Jeff on the Star Voyager and Roger on the orbital station was seamless, bridging the gap created by the distance and the communication delays. Together, they navigated through the intricate repair process, each step meticulously executed under Roger's guidance.

As the final adjustments were made, the spacecraft's systems began to stabilize. The alarms ceased their urgent wailing, and the flashing red lights were replaced by the steady glow of normal operation. They had done it. Against all odds, and with Roger's crucial assistance, they had saved the Star Voyager from disaster

.Jeff let out a sigh of relief, a mixture of exhaustion and triumph washing over him. Greta turned to him, a proud smile on her face. "Well done, Jeff. You handled that brilliantly."

As they thanked Roger and signed off, the weight of the crisis they had just averted settled on them. It was a stark reminder of the dangers of space travel, but also a testament to the power of teamwork and clear communication. The Star Voyager continued on its journey, its crew stronger and more united than ever before. The adventure, with all its challenges and uncertainties, was still unfolding, and they were ready to face whatever lay ahead.

The Star Voyager, now steady and secure after the harrowing crisis, continued on its journey through the vast expanse of space. The experience had been a profound one for both Captain Greta Proton and Jeff Reynolds, not just in terms of the technical challenge they overcame but also in the invaluable lesson they learned about communication.

As the spacecraft glided through the cosmos, the incident with the life support system remained a topic of reflection for the crew. Greta, with her years of experience, had seen her fair share of challenges in space.

However, this particular situation highlighted an aspect often overlooked in the realm of space exploration and, indeed, in any technical field: the critical importance of clear communication.

Jeff, who had felt the weight of the crisis most acutely, realized how easily things could have spiraled out of control. The jargon-laden instructions from Earth, coupled with the frustrating time delays, had nearly cost them dearly. It was Roger's clear, jargon-free communication that had made the difference, transforming a near-disaster into a success.

This realization brought a new perspective to the mission. As they journeyed back to Earth, Greta and Jeff spent time reviewing their procedures and communication protocols. They knew that in space, as in many customer-oriented fields, clear and straightforward communication was not just a matter of convenience; it was often a matter of survival.

Greta shared her insights with the mission control team upon their return. "In space, every second counts. Complex jargon and communication delays can be more than just frustrating; they can be deadly," she explained. "We must ensure that our instructions are clear and accessible to all team members, regardless of their expertise level."

Jeff echoed her sentiments, adding his personal experience to the discussion. "As someone who was on the receiving end of those instructions, I can't emphasize enough the importance of clarity. It's not just about understanding the problem; it's about being able to act quickly and efficiently to solve it."

Questions for the reader

Do you communicate to customers in real time, or rely on relays?
Is your jargon helpful internally, but making critical situations more difficult for your customers to navigate?

Waves of Demand

In Wavecrest, a beach town where the sun glistened on the ocean like diamonds and waves whispered of adventure, Chairman Boogie Boards stood as a symbol of seaside exhilaration. Renowned for their top-quality boogie boards, the company embarked on a new venture, crafting surfboards. This bold move, filled with promise, was about to test the company's resilience in unexpected ways.

Jimmy Boardshorts was not just the pride of Wavecrest; he was its heart and soul, a figure synonymous with the spirit of surfing. As the reigning champion of the Big Wave Competition, his connection with the ocean went far beyond the realm of sport.

It was a bond shaped by the legacy of his grandfather, a legendary surfer whose tales of the sea had been Jimmy's bedtime stories. These tales had instilled in him an unwavering respect for the ocean's power and beauty. Surfing for Jimmy was a part of his identity and a rhythm that pulsed in his veins.

In anticipation of the upcoming competition, Jimmy had committed himself to a goal that went beyond retaining his title. He had taken up an extra job, working long hours to save enough money to purchase Chairman's newly launched surfboard.

The decision to buy this board was not made lightly; it was a testament to his trust in a brand that had become a symbol of quality and innovation in the world of surfing. He saw this new board as a worthy successor to the one that had carried him to victory in the past, a vessel that would help continue his legacy.

His faith in Chairman was so strong that he made a generous, albeit risky, decision. As the competition neared and his new board had not yet arrived, he decided to lend his old, trusted surfboard to his younger brother, Timmy.

Timmy, a budding surfer with dreams of his own, had long idolized Jimmy and aspired to follow in his footsteps. The act of passing on his board to Timmy was more than a gesture of brotherly love; it was a reflection of Jimmy's confidence in Chairman's promise to deliver the new surfboard on time. It was a decision made in the belief that he would not be left without a board for the competition, a belief rooted in the trust he had in a company that had been an integral part of his surfing journey.

This choice, however, was laced with a poignant irony. The very trust that led Jimmy to support his brother's aspirations also exposed him to the vulnerability of disappointment. The new surfboard, bought with hard-earned money and awaited with bated breath, became a symbol of unfulfilled expectations, a stark reminder of the distance between corporate promises and the passionate hopes of those who ride the waves.

At Chairman's manufacturing hub, Doug Sax navigated his own sea of challenges. A former surfer whose career was cut short by an injury, Doug had found a new purpose at Chairman. He rose through the ranks, his surfer's soul enriching his role as Plant Manager. He understood the essence of a board, the thrill of riding a wave, making him not just an efficient manager but also a custodian of dreams.

The surfboard launch triggered an unprecedented demand, overwhelming even the most optimistic forecasts. Doug, balancing the company's cautious financial approach with practicality, faced a significant dilemma. Opting to prioritize demand, he authorized using materials reserved for boogie boards for surfboard production. This decision, though strategic, led to a backlog in boogie board orders, stirring discontent among loyal customers.

As the Big Wave Competition neared, Jimmy Boardshorts' anticipation was eclipsed by a profound sense of disappointment. The surfboard he had eagerly awaited from Chairman, a company he had revered for years, was a letdown. While its design was visually striking, capturing the essence of the sea and the spirit of surfing, its performance was a stark contrast to its appearance.

It lacked the agility, the responsiveness, and the resilience that were the hallmarks of Chairman's products. This board, which he had hoped would be a new companion on the waves, felt alien under his feet, unresponsive to the dance of the surf that he so loved. Feeling let down by a brand that was almost a part of his identity, Jimmy reached out to Chairman's customer service. Adrienne, known for her empathy and problem-solving skills, answered his call.

As Jimmy voiced his concerns, there was a tremor of frustration in his voice, a sense of betrayal that went beyond mere dissatisfaction with a product. This board was supposed to be his partner in defending his title, a symbol of his connection with the ocean.

Adrienne, recognizing the depth of Jimmy's disillusionment, offered a replacement board and a Chairman-branded t-shirt as a gesture of goodwill. However, to Jimmy, this offer seemed almost trivial in comparison to what he was losing. A t-shirt was a paltry consolation for missing out on the competition, an event that was not just a contest for him but a celebration of his lifelong passion for surfing. The delay in receiving a board of the expected quality meant that he would not be able to compete, to defend his title, to be part of the event that he had looked forward to all year. The competition was a part of his identity, a testament to his skill and his bond with the sea.

The notion of receiving a t-shirt in exchange for this significant loss felt almost insulting. It was a stark reminder of the disconnect between the corporate decisions and the passions of those who lived for the sport.

 For a company like Chairman, which had built its reputation on understanding and catering to surfers' needs, this misstep was not just a simple mistake; it was a fundamental oversight of what their products meant to their customers.

In that moment, Jimmy's disappointment in Chairman Boogie Boards deepened. It wasn't just about a surfboard; it was about a trust that had been broken, a bond that had been taken for granted. The company's failure to deliver a product that lived up to its reputation had resulted in more than just a material loss for Jimmy. It had cost him a part of his surfing soul, a chapter in his story that would now remain unwritten.

Meanwhile, Doug confronted the emerging quality issues head-on. The new supplier, though prompt, had provided substandard materials, compromising the surfboards' integrity. This was against everything Doug and Chairman stood for, prompting a drastic but necessary response.

Amidst his disappointment, Timmy offered to return Jimmy's board. Jimmy displayed remarkable selflessness, telling his younger brother that it was his turn to try for the cup. Timmy, often in Jimmy's shadow, saw this as an opportunity to forge his path. Inspired by his brother's gesture, he approached the competition with a mix of anticipation and determination.

The Big Wave Competition was a spectacle of skill and spirit. Without his new board, Jimmy made a tough decision to withdraw, focusing instead on supporting Timmy. The competition was a whirlwind of talent, but Timmy stood out. He caught a monstrous wave, riding a tube with an expertise that belied his experience. Then, in a breathtaking move, he executed a flawless backflip off the crest, landing smoothly and drawing cheers from the awestruck crowd. This incredible display clinched Timmy's victory.

In a heartwarming moment, Jimmy, brimming with pride, handed the trophy to Timmy. The younger Boardshorts took a celebratory photo with the trophy and, ironically, a SurfRunner board – Chairman's main rival in the Surfboard market.

This image, capturing both triumph and subtle irony, resonated deeply with the crowd, including Doug, who was among them. Witnessing SurfRunner bask in the limelight, Doug felt a pang of regret but also a renewed sense of purpose.

The feedback from Jimmy and other customers, coupled with the competition's events, spurred Chairman to action. Doug led the charge in reevaluating their processes, focusing on quality, and reestablishing their commitment to the surfing community.

The decision to recall the affected surfboards and replace them was expensive, but reflected their dedication to excellence and customer satisfaction.

Chairman's journey through this crisis was transformative. They emerged stronger, more attuned to their community, and with a renewed commitment to uphold the surfing legacy.

The story of the Boardshorts brothers became a symbol of hope and resilience, a reminder of the impact one company, and its products, can have on lives and dreams. In the end, the waves of Wavecrest witnessed not just the rise of a young surfer but the unbreakable bond of brotherhood and the enduring spirit of a community united by the love of the ocean.

Questions for the Reader
Has your organization ever sacrificed a core value in a time of crisis?
Did you win a battle by almost losing the war?

Conclusion

As we conclude our journey through the wild and whimsical world of business, it is clear that the most memorable lessons often come from the most unexpected places. From feeding sloths to meatball rivalries, each chapter of this book has presented a bizarre yet insightful look into the heart of business wisdom.

In "Feeding the Sloth," we learned that simplicity often trumps complexity, and sometimes the best solution is to meet our challenges (or our sloths) halfway. "Meatball Management" showed us the delicate balance between cost-cutting and maintaining quality, proving that sometimes the secret ingredient is just good, old-fashioned common sense.

The adventures at Oceanic Voyages in "Turning the Ship Around" highlighted the importance of aligning sales and fulfillment, reminding us that the best business strategies are those where everyone is paddling in the same direction. "The AutoDream Nightmare" served as a cautionary tale about the pitfalls of digitalization without careful planning, underscoring the need for meticulous attention to operational details.

Our corporate canoe race in "Up the Creek with Two Working Paddles" illustrated the perils of ignoring fundamental problems. It was a soggy reminder that sometimes the biggest obstacle to success is our own reluctance to address the underlying issues.

Finally with "Jargonauts", Captain Greta Proton and rookie astronaut Jeff Reynolds embark on a historic space journey aboard the Star Voyager, only to face a critical life support system failure due to a complex electrical fault. Jargon proves to be the opposite of helpful, and communication delays are anything but out of this world.

In this book, we have seen that the absurdities of business can often mirror the absurdities of life. The lessons are clear: embrace simplicity, focus on quality, align your team's efforts, pay attention to the details, address fundamental problems, and manage expectations. But most importantly, don't forget to laugh along the way. After all, a sense of humor might just be the most valuable asset in your business toolkit.

So, as you close this book, remember that the next time you face a business dilemma, you might just find your solution in the most unexpected of places - perhaps even while feeding a sloth or flying your spaceship. Keep your eyes open, your mind sharp, and your funny bone tickled. Business, like life, is a journey best enjoyed with a smile.

About the author

A self-confessed dad joke aficionado, Joe's humor is as predictable as it is groan-inducing. Joe is a publisher with a dynamic background encompassing banking, insurance, sales, and operations, Joe's experiences drive the characters in his stories. Whether he's negotiating book deals, helping an author navigate customs fees in Gambia, or navigating the canyons of Southern Utah, Joe can be found concocting puns that bring smiles and eye-rolls in equal measure.

Joe's philosophy on meals: the best food is the one currently on the plate. In essence, a storyteller at heart, a humorist in spirit, and an adventurer by nature. His life, much like his jokes, is a testament to finding joy in every moment and laughter in every corner. His approach to life blends humor, curiosity, and a relentless pursuit of the next great adventure, whether in publishing or on the hiking trail. Joe calls the Red Cliffs of Southern Utah home.